Wilson Reading System®

Dictation Book
Steps 1-6

WILSON®

Wilson works.

THIRD EDITION

by Barbara A. Wilson

Wilson Language Training Corporation
175 West Main Street
Millbury, MA 01527
www.wilsonlanguage.com

Wilson Reading System® Dictation Book Steps 1-6

Item # WRSD16

ISBN 1-56778-053-9

THIRD EDITION (revised)

The Wilson Reading System is published by:

Wilson Language Training Corporation
175 West Main Street
Millbury, MA 01527
United States of America

(508) 865-5699

www.wilsonlanguage.com

Printed in the U.S.A.

Introduction

The **Dictation Book** contains the very controlled word presentation inherent to the entire Wilson Reading System. The words included in this book are appropriate for the spelling portion of a lesson, Parts 6-8.

The **WRS Instructor Manual** fully describes the method of teaching each of the concepts. The **WRS Rules Notebook** contains sounds and rules taught at each step.

Reading and spelling are opposite processes. Sounds and rules for reading must be presented for spelling as well. Therefore, to be most effective, this Dictation Book should be used in conjunction with the entire Wilson Reading System. However, selected students may primarily need spelling. For students using the program for spelling only, Parts 1, 2, 6, 7 and 8 of the lesson plan should be followed.

At the beginning of each step, there is a "What Says" page. The number of responses will increase as new sounds are taught and **new responses** appear in **bold print**. For example, a student is asked, "What says /**z**/?" In substep 1.2, the response is **z** (see page 2). In substep 1.6, the answer is **z** and **s**, (sometimes as a suffix). In substep 4.1, the response becomes **z** and sometimes **s**, sometimes as a suffix or between two vowels (see the "What Says" page Step 4).

The words in small print between lines at the top of each sentence list can be spelled for the students as needed. At the end of each substep, new sight words are presented to the student to memorize. This list is at the end of the Rules Notebook. The student should make a sight word dictionary and enter the new words into it when they are presented to him. The Instructor Manual describes the manner used to teach sight words.

If any part of a word is underlined, it may be 'given' to the student. For example, for the Step 1 word **kid**, students may be told that the /**k**/ sound is made with a **k**, rather than a **c**. Later in Step 7, the student will learn the rules for **c**, **k** sound options. Other examples of underlined clues for students include capitalization and nonsense syllables.

"What Says?"

Consonant Phonemes

1.1

/s/ - s	/d/ - d	/f/ - f
/m/ - m	/g/ - g	/l/ - l
/r/ - r	/p/ - p	/n/ - n
/t/ - t		

1.2

/b/ - b	/ks/ - x	/sh/ - sh
/y/ - y	/h/ - h	/z/ - z
/j/ - j	/ch/ - ch	/k/ - c, k, ck
/th/ - th	/v/ - v	/kw/ - qu
/w/ - w, wh	/hw/ - wh	

1.6

/z/ - z, s (sometimes as a suffix)

Vowel Phonemes

1.1

/ă/ - a	/ĭ/ - i	/ŏ/ - o

1.2

/ŭ/ - u	/ĕ/ - e

Additional Sounds

1.4

/ȯl/ - all

1.5

/am/ - am	/an/ - an

the had a did on is his he

a	*s, m, r (initial)*	*d, g, p, t (final)*		
sad	sat	sap	mad	mat
map	rat	rag	rap	

The rat is mad.

The rat sat on the mat.

The rat had a rag.

---

f,l,n (initial)

| lap | lad | lag | nap | nag |
| Nat | fat | at | | |

The lad is sad.

Is the fat rat on his lap?

The rag is on the mat.

The rat had a nap.

Nat is sad.

The lad had the map.

---

i

| rip | rid | rig | lip | lit |
| lid | sip | sit | fit | it |

The rag had a rip.

Did Sid sit on the map?

The lid fit.

Is Nat mad at Sid?

Sid had a nap on the mat.

---

o

| rod | rot | not | nod | lot |
| log | fog | on | Rod | mop |

It is not a rat.

Rod sat on the log.

Sid had the mop.

Did the log rot?

The map is on his lap.

He is not on the lot.

1.2 A

	is	had	a	the	of	to	I	from	her	his	this	and	has	like	will	he	was

b (final) | *sh*

mob	nab	sob	rib	fib
lab	rob	lob	fish	lash
rash	shot	shop	mash	ship

Rob had a rash.

The ship had fish on it.

I had to shop.

u

lug	mug	rut	rush	sun
run	mud	sub		

Sid is in a rush.

Rob sat in the sun.

Rob had a sip from the mug.

b, d, g, p, t (initial)

pig	pit	pat	tap	tag
top	dog	dot	dig	bag
bat	gap	gash	got	big
bit	bug	gum	pot	pad
dash	tug	bud	tot	tip
dish	pup	bus	dug	but
dad	bad	bun	pop	

a, i, o, u | *b, d, f, g, l, m, n, p, r, s, t, sh*

The dog had a dish of fish.

The bug is in the pot.

Pat had a pig in the pit.

Did Nat run to the shop?

The pup sat in the sun.

The tot got gum on the rug.

Sal got a lot of fish.

The bus is in a rut.

Did the dog dig the pit?

Dash to the shop!

The gum is in the bag.

Dad had a bad rash.

The bat is on his lap.

Rob bit the fig.

Mom had a sip of pop.

Did Dad mop the shop?

---

h, j

hop	hit	hush	hat	hot
hip	hid	hog	had	job
jug	jot	jut	jab	Jim
jig	jog	jag		

Jim got the job on the ship.

Did mom jog to the shop?

The tot hid the hat.

---

c, k

cat	cub	cash	<u>K</u>im	cab
cot	cup	<u>k</u>id	cut	cob
cap	cod	cop	<u>K</u>it	

c, k

Kim had the cat on her lap.

Dad had a nap on the cot.

Did Jim cut his lip on this cup?

---

ck

lock	duck	back	pack	Nick
luck	sick	rock	puck	Rick
sock	tack	rack	Dick	tick
pick	lick	sack		

Rick sat on the big rock.

Kim had bad luck.

The duck is back on the ship.

---

e

met	Meg	fed	let	leg
led	red	set	pet	Ben
bed	bet	beg	neck	shed
get				

Meg fed her pet cat.

Ben sat on the deck.

Deb met her dad.

Pat led the pup to his dish.

Kit had a bad cut on her leg.

Rick had to rush to get the bus.

Meg had a red hat.

Let the cat lick the dish.

Jim and Ben met in the shop.

The duck is on the dock.

Did Kim jog with Mom?

Get Rick the sock on the rug.

Dick and the dog got on the bus.

v, w, x, y, z

wag	wig	wish	vat	vet
Viv	zip	zag	zap	wet
yet	yes	fox	tax	box
wax	tux	Max		

Did Jack wax his hot rod?

I wish Max had a dog.

Yes, the wig is on Viv.

ch, th

chop	rich	Chet	chip	chin
chap	chat	such	Seth	Beth
bath	thin	path	thick	thud
with	math	thug		

Did Beth chop the log?

Chet had such fun with the pup.

Did Jim jog on the path?

qu, wh

quick	quack	quiz	quit	whip
when	whiz	whop	which	

Did Rick go to the vet?

Dick had a chat with Dad.

I wish that I had the quiz.

Is Jack in his tux?

The fox is in the pen.

Quick, run to get the wig!

Did that duck quack?

He was a <u>wh</u>iz on that quiz.

I wish to jog on that path.

Tom is thin.

That pup had a hot bath.

Dad has a box of gum.

1.3 A Words

mop	rib	sob	jog	rash
map	rock	cop	such	dot
lid	mud	Ted	fix	lap
web	not	lick	much	ten
chip	tub	bed	moth	at
hip	lock	peg	shot	had
rich	bug	pen	bat	hit
pet	lash	bus	bun	pick
path	bib	red	jab	kid
nod	but	cup	mix	pot
Ben	kick	pat	tick	tab
Jim	tin	cob	rat	big
tip	cot	Rick	dash	whip
mad	den	gum	math	neck
dip	mug	sub	dish	wig
yes	fun	this	zip	sick
tug	thin	cub	fit	shut
rush	wish	quit	back	pup
fog	shop	lot	hut	pack
sit				

1.3 A Words (continued)

let	gap	fish	sip	dug
dig	cab	Sid	Dick	vet
wax	chin	sock	shed	led
mat	lit	pig	nap	<u>ki</u>t
Jack	then	job	did	zap
rub	ship	tot	pad	zag
rug	them	pal	fox	nut
gas	him			

1.3 B Words

chug	vat	dab	pub	con
hub	sash	dim	pod	tax
dock	sag	lab	Sis	pin
pun	quip	hack	fib	shin
mod	deck	chub	yen	quiz
chum	nick	sod	posh	yap
pug	thud	lack	bob	hut
shag	tick	bud	hex	bog
hag	mob	hush	peck	hash
bid	sum	lush	rack	pod
lad	bin	dud	nog	rap
jack	cod	lag	vim	hem
wick	nun	<u>ki</u>n	lug	<u>whi</u>z
sack	sin	rid	fin	nag
nab	gal	rum	mesh	

1.3 B Words (continued)

rig	shod	thug	rim	jut
tux	chat	lax	gut	kit
chap	sop	shim	ped	cad
rut	fad	gag	keg	jot
gun	gap	tog	lox	gab
lob	whim	wit	bop	<u>wh</u>ack
shun	jag	chuck	shuck	shock

1.3 Nonsense

sut	vid	weg	zat	dep
pob	dem	vib	sot	lix
quib	yut	jeb	zeg	fub
gad	quop	med	dex	jid
ret	fap	piz	lig	wog
quat	jit	lub	hup	vin
gaz	min	dob	vob	wex
riz	tup	jux	dap	zib
foz	fif	squim	tex	bup
sep	jum	rop	bish	lat
quap	chib	huz	feg	sith
quet	wup	tez	fep	rem
gup	rab	dax	choz	tem
poth	mip	yim	jup	bep
hosh	dith	wib	yeb	fash
gom	vash	bix	jud	chep
dop	mish	thez	lod	

and   for   to   he   is   the   his   a   from   does   has

Tim hid the cat.

The fish is hot.

Tim has the mop and the rag.

Tom got the big job.

Tim had a nap.

Bob has a cut on his lip.

Beth had a wig and a hat.

Ted met Bev at the shop.

A big moth is in the pot.

Did Rick hop on that bus?

Jack did a jig on the rug.

Mom got the tot a bib.

Did Tom nab the fish?

Tim had a sip of pop.

Did the dog nip Pat?

Beth had to get the bus.

Ted got in the tub and had a bath.

Bob led the dog to the dish.

Rick had a dot on his chin.

The pen is in the den.

The pig bit the hog.

The cat got the rat.

Bob sat on the big cot.

Did Chet wish for a pup?

Bob got in the tub for a bath.

That kid is sad.

Tim hit his chin.

It is a cub on the path!

Mom got fish at the shop.

Tom got the gum on the rug.

Jim can jog on the path.

Tim got a nip from the pup.

Tom got a dish for his dog.

Ben let the dog on his bed.

Ted did not get the fish.

Tim fed the cat six fish!

Sid sat in the hot tub.

The fox got the hen.

Peg did not get the pig.

Dad let Chet pack the bag.

Rick had a bad cut on his leg.

The hen is in the shed.

Ed got the fish with his net.

Did the dog lick Ben on his neck?

Don dug a pit in the mud.

Did the dog wag and yap?

I wish to get that hat back.

Get the bug in the web.

1.3 B Sentences

for   will   I   from   would   Mr.   Ms.   Mrs.   of   the   a   is   his   to   and   a.m.

Yes, Meg had to jog on that path.

Tom hit Jim in the rib.

Did Tom get the job at the sub shop?

I will hush the mob.

Pat is a rich kid.

Dad did not get much cash for the job.

Jim is in the shed with Jack.

Pat will jog in the fog.

The rim of this pot is hot.

Tom got the map from the cab.

It is at the lab.

Bob and Jim will mop the rig.

Ben is such a nag at the shop.

Beth led Tom to the dock.

Did the vet dip the dog in the tick bath?

A yak dug in wet sod for a fig.

Kim will rip the top of the rag.

Tom will jog on the path to the hut.

This job is big, but it is fun.

Mom did not nag Pat.

Chad had a nap on the cot.

The tot got a hug from his mom.

Tom got a lug nut for the job.

The thug hit Jim in the gut.

Dick will chop the logs in the back of the hut.

Meg and Bob sat and had a chat.

Beth had to get to the job at ten.

Chet is mad at Beth.

Don got mud on his hot rod.

Ed had bad jet lag.

Ed did dash to the shop.

Ben is in a rut with his job.

Did Pat get a bad rap?

The vet had a shot for the dog.

Tom quit the job at the ship.

When did Beth get lax with the job?

That tax on gas is not bad.

Did Jed lack vim for the job?

Bob got up to wax the hot rod.

The Red Sox had to win!

Mr. Quin is on the deck.

Max got six fish with his rod.

The fox got the hen in the pen.

Did Ms. Lin get the bus at ten a.m.?

1.4 A Words

shell	cuff	fuss	miss	kiss
off	fill	puff	toss	doll
hill	fell	chill	Russ	Bess
well	mess	Nell	mass	bell
pill	will	huff	wall	fall
hall	call	ball	tall	mall

1.4 B Words

dull	chess	moss	mull	dill
mill	buff	bill	hiss	miff
sill	muff	lass	lull	joss
till	mall			

1.4 Nonsense

thill	poff	fass	raff	tuss
yill	poss	sull	siff	vell
jull	goss	hoff	liss	vull
hess	chull	daff	kell	niff
wess	zuff	rass	lill	rull
sess	faff	zall	biss	

1.4 A Sentences

her I has been for and is his

I will huff and puff up the big hill.

Bill has been sick.

Did Chet get the red shell?

Bess had a big kiss for her dad.

Beth sat in the den with Bill.

Tim will fill the dish with fish.

Bill had to mop up the mess.

The bug fell in the web.

Did Dad yell at Tom?

Bev got a chill in the tub.

Jack had to sell his pig.

Ed will kill the big bug.

This hall is a mess!

Mom did not miss the mud at all.

Sid fell on the path.

Toss the ball to Kim.

Will Jill and Russ go to the mall?

Can you call the pup?

Bess will go to the mall.

Dad had the red ball for Jen.

1.4 B Sentences

from   I   she   for   is

Did Jill hiss at the bad dog?

Dad will fill the cup with Tab.

Ben had fun with the lass.

Ted will not jog in this fog.

Bob had a big kiss from Meg.

Will Liz get that dull job?

I bet Nell will pass in math.

The lass will get the bill at the pub.

Did Rick pass the hot rod?

The lass hid on the hill.

Did Jim miss Pat?

The pot on the sill is in the sun.

The boss got a bell for the shop.

Jeff did not yell at the tot.

Sal got Liz a chess set at the West Mall.

I bet that job is dull.

Sid fell in the hall.

1.5 A Words

ham	Sam	can	than	pan
man	fan	Jan	am	jam
Dan	tan	Pam		

1.5 B Words

sham	ban	bam	dam	ram
yam				

1.5 Nonsense

zam	lan	tiv	zat	vam
laz	han	bap	hud	kem
yex	yan	roff	quam	fam
heg	gop	zan	kep	lib
bam	cax	san	jun	quan
yab	pesh	tham	shan	cham

1.5 A Sentences

for   and

Jill can nap on the bed.

Dan sat in the pig pen!

The dog ran on the path.

Pat hid the jam in the shed.

Did Beth get the fan for the den?

Sam will get in the tub for a bath.

The ram on the hill is big.

Ben had a red and tan hat.

Pam and Bob had fun at the mill.

Sam has a bad rash on his leg.

1.5 B Sentences

Did Pam get that wig at the shop?

Dad will dash to get the ham.

The moth fell in the yam.

I am sad about the loss.

Can Liz and Rich do the job?

Ed and Tom will jam in the shed.

Dan had to rush the pup to a vet.

The man got a cash tip for the job.

Mash that yam in the pan.

Seth had ham with his egg.

1.6 A Words

dogs	pens	pups	shops	locks
webs	nets	pegs	hams	chins
backs	mats	mills	chills	maps
tops	sips	wets	bills	rubs
necks	bells	lugs	shuts	rugs
shells	fans	tins	<u>k</u>icks	huffs
sheds	wins	pins	runs	fills
nuts	packs	jugs	sits	bugs
pats	zags	naps	tubs	buds
sets	fibs	dads	socks	pills
chips	ships	dabs	<u>k</u>ids	paths
pits	cans	quits	zaps	rocks
cops	lips	mops	tugs	beds
bets				

1.6 B Words

subs	<u>k</u>its	<u>wh</u>ips	puns	mobs
docks	yams	bins	nags	pecks
lads	chums	robs	yells	racks
thugs	sums	yens	decks	peds
rigs	quills	rots	lacks	dubs
jabs	hags	huts		

1.6 Nonsense

zups	wegs	baps	mips	cheds
tods	duts	sans	lems	rills
jops	kigs	gans	vams	shids
thons	wubs	pabs	hets	foms
whibs	chots	biffs	daths	zums
shens	mabs	thubs	nugs	mons
squims	zans	luns	dods	jegs
sibs	qualls	rabs	fums	chims
heffs	shobs	whabs	puds	chigs
tibs	queds	gogs	yats	juffs
thims	valls	yans	futs	fams
thigs				

1.6 A Sentences

for   are   Mr.

Dad sits in the den with his pet dog.

The <u>k</u>ids will nap on the cot.

Tim got the mops in the shed.

The rugs had lots of mud on them.

Mr. Quin yells at the <u>k</u>ids.

Seth runs to the dock with Tom.

Ben sells dolls in his shop.

The shells are red.

Chet lugs the jug up the hill.

Pam hugs the pup when it is sad.

Mom nods to Jim to get Sis.

Tom runs such a rush.

Fill the cups for the <u>k</u>ids.

Ted will mop the decks.

The ship gets lots of sun.

The dolls are in the van.

Dan shops at the mall.

Sam has ticks.

The kids get chips at the shop.

Mom fills the jugs in the shed.

Bob naps in the den on the rug.

Jim has bags of shells.

Chet gabs to Jill.

The <u>k</u>ids had the ball in the bin.

Fill the jug with the nuts.

The dog runs with Tim.

Did Rick get the bells for the shop?

The red pens are on the bed.

Mom nods to Jim to get Sis.

Tom runs to the bus in such a rush.

Fill the cups with Tab for the <u>k</u>ids.

Seth will mop the decks and the hall.

The decks of the ship get lots of sun.

I miss my chums at the shop.

The hub caps are in the van.

Dan shops at the mall with Will.

Beth lugs the mops and rags.

The maps are not in the cab.

Viv is nuts about Bill!

Ed bops at the bash and has fun.

The thug got hub caps off the van.

Sid quits a job if it is not fun.

Ben jabs the bag and then jogs.

The boss gets Beth to do the job.

Did the cops get the <u>k</u>ids in the hot rod?

Bill nags Tom to fix the van.

Meg gets the chills.

The fans yell for Nick at bat.

"What Says?"

Consonant Phonemes

2.1 - 2.5

/b/ - b	/p/ - p	/d - d
/kw/ - qu	/f/ - f	/r/ - r
/g/ - g	/s/ - s	/h/ - h
/t/ - t	/j/ - j	/v/ - v
/k/ - c, k, ck	/w/ - w, wh	/l/ - l
/ks/ - x	/m/ - m	/y/ - y
/n/ - n	/z/ - z, s (sometimes as a suffix)	/ch/ - ch
/th/ - th	/sh/ - sh	/hw/ - wh

Vowel Phonemes

2.1 - 2.5

/ă/ - a	/ĕ/ - e	/ĭ/ - i
/ŏ/ - o	/ŭ/ - u	

Additional Sounds

2.1

/ȯl/ - all	**/ang/ - ang**	**/ank/ - ank**
/am/ - am	**/ing/ - ing**	**/ink/ - ink**
/an/ - an	**/ong/ - ong**	**/onk/ - onk**
	/ung/ - ung	**/unk/ - unk**

2.3

/īld/ - ild	**/ōld/ - old**	**/ōst/ - ost**
/īnd/ - ind	**/ōlt/ - olt**	

2.1 A Words

ng, nk

bang	ring	sang	long	song
lung	king	wing	hang	sing
fang	hung	thing	rang	sung
pink	honk	sank	think	junk
rink	sink	thank	tank	chunk
bank	dunk	link	bunk	Hank
sunk	wink	banks	rings	things
honks	wings	hangs	kings	thinks
winks	sings	fangs	rinks	sinks
thanks	tanks	chunks	lungs	bunks
songs				

2.1 B Words

ng, nk

shank	rank	gong	tong	zing
mink	rung	song	hunk	pang
kink	lank	yank	punk	funk
bonk	dung	fink	zonk	gang
gunk	tang	ranks	gongs	zings
minks	rungs	hunks	yanks	tongs
shanks	dunks	links		

2.1 Nonsense

ng, nk

zung	hink	gank	fank	ting
wung	vong	cang	zunk	fong
hing	jank	jong	fing	lonk
lunk	pank	jing	zang	ying
tunk	bink	quink	quang	mank
shing	thunk			

2.1 A Sentences

are   for   my   or

ng, nk

Tom sang the song to the kids.

Get the ping-pong balls.

Bob has bad lungs.

It is a long run up the hill.

Kim will sing at the shop.

Did Bob hang this up?

The king has had bad luck.

The ring did not fit Meg.

What is the thing in this jug?

Thank Dad for the gum.

Ed sank the shot to win!

The cat got a big chunk of fish.

Mom had Ben get rid of the junk.

The wings on the bug are pink.

Jim had the top bunk for his nap.

The ship sank in the bath tub.

The kids are at the rink.

My cash is in the bank.

2.1 B Sentences

from   for   so   you

ng, nk

Dad had a wink for Pam.

Hank had to get the map for Tom.

I will thank Ed for the mink.

Jim did not think of his job at all.

It is such a long jog up the hill.

I think that Bill has the top rank.

Did Bess bang on the gong?

ng, nk

Pat is not a punk.

Jim will dunk the ball in the net.

Ben had a big chunk of gum for the kids.

Did Bill yank the hat from Tom?

The cab had to honk at the bus.

The cops had the link to get the con man.

Jim had so much junk on his bed.

Jan hung the mink in the den.

Did the man sing six songs?

Ben had a ring for Jill.

I will hang this up for you.

Get the things in the den for Sam.

Bob had to fill the gas tank.

Yank the ball from the pup.

2.2 A Words

sent	must	best	lend	drop
loft	pest	pond	flap	crib
bent	grab	jump	bend	chest
last	dent	trash	raft	stub
gust	grip	clock	brag	flop
stash	belt	stuck	cost	glad
grin	crab	plug	sand	drum
slush	trot	wept	dust	rest
hunt	vest	step	flag	swish
drag	drip	black	past	stick
vent	dump	ramp	brush	

fist	bunch	task	flip	test
click	camp	frog	crack	spin
soft	fast	squish	trap	crash
cloth	thump	stack	lost	nest
bled	mast	next	list	snip
spot	limp	block	lump	damp
clam	skin	flock	crop	plan
flat	west	snap	hint	cluck
blush	ranch	skip	pluck	kept
bench	clap	fled	chimp	small
mask	crush	pinch	band	punch
chomp	pump	clip	mint	slam
twig	shrug	trim	munch	rust
mend	slim	scab	melt	shelf
felt	help	silk	golf	milk
gulf	self	tilt	film	gulp
held	wilt	smog	flash	stop
snug	shrub	pant	went	just
gift	Fran	Brad	swim	glass
cross	press	spell	grass	fluff
class	dress	bless	still	stuff
cliff	drill	sniff	spill	drops
ponds	pests	dents	stubs	grips
clocks	plugs	drums	vests	steps
flags	drags	drips	flips	tests
clicks	camps	frogs	cracks	stacks

scan	wh<u>i</u><u>s</u>k	vast	fund	rasp
stun	stock	crux	plod	fend
shaft	cram	fret	grid	rapt
blab	duct	sift	flex	pomp
clot	scum	blot	stag	glen
flax	rant	brim	shred	prod
frock	cast	tact	sect	glob
rift	scat	tuft	clod	slat
flab	snob	flux	blob	zest
s<u>k</u>id	romp	flit	crock	pact
gasp	tint	span	mist	tend
slot	disc	grub	quest	finch
prop	snag	facts	losh	bond
trod	slug	slob	loft	brash
wimp	prep	deft	flub	slab
fleck	fond	dis<u>k</u>	clop	chant
<u>wh</u>elp	helm	belch	sul<u>k</u>	cult
pelt	hul<u>k</u>	filth	hilt	<u>k</u>elp
jilt	meld	silt	bul<u>k</u>	pulp
stall	clad	sped	hemp	prom
lint	clog	slit	squall	tus<u>k</u>
brat	bust	clack	bulb	Welsh
ris<u>k</u>	weld	plot	speck	glum
dus<u>k</u>	yelp	flick	lisp	vamp

2.2 B Words (continued)

bas<u>k</u>	hus<u>k</u>	dwell	gruff	thrill
bluff	skull	brass	swell	staff
gloss	Swiss	bliss	shrill	floss
crass	slots	grubs	quests	props
snags	bonds	slugs	slobs	lofts
wimps	slabs	flecks	spans	gasps
chants	sul<u>k</u>s	cults	pelts	tints

2.2 Nonsense

flup	glip	dret	frish	spag
dren	chent	flod	plog	hist
zimp	plosh	brez	frex	clom
preb	shont	freb	ploth	grud
stim	trug	gren	frib	stish
droth	drap	trit	zent	drob
plon	vunt	chust	rimp	gruth
speff	thisk	slith	shomp	gret
pelf	blid	hilk	doft	shusp
fent	grad	spad	flam	bloss
clab	plen	chelp	blass	plud
clim	masp	prab	quist	fliss
gleff	triz	clug	trop	hest
plix	cliz	priz	quelt	

you   from   for   my   we   so   about   her   go

The belt is on the shelf in the den.

Did Beth step on that frog?

This clock is the best gift!

Bill fell in the wet sand.

Stan must dump the trash.

Ted will jump in the pond and swim.

Mom will mend the rip in the dress.

I wish that <u>K</u>im did not brag.

Ben went on the ship.

The class must get a flag.

Tim will get the cloth on the shelf.

Pass the small block to Jed.

Jill had the plum.

Bob went with Dad to the ranch.

The tot fell in the wet slush.

Bob had the last mint.

Trot up to the flag and then run.

Ben got a cut on his leg from the trap.

Beth had a pink sil<u>k</u> dress.

Did Tom brag about his six big fish?

Get the trash to the dump.

We will hunt for the lost raft.

Stan will lift that big pump.

Did Tom trip on that twig?

I held my pup as he got a shot.

Brad is sick so he can not help.

Bill is at the swim club with Tom.

Jan got the drill for her dad.

We will trim the tall grass.

Ben will sell the clams.

This pink shell was on the sand.

Did the dog sniff the fish?

It was fun to go on that trip!

The kids dug in the soft sand.

Dad was cross about the mess.

Did Ed win at golf?

Did the ball swish in the net?

Gram will mend the vest.

Grab a lunch and go to the pond.

Jill will get the doll in the crib.

Do not dump that stuff on the bed!

Tom sets up drums for the band.

Jim must not miss that class.

Stan must sit on the bench.

The twin wept.

Fran will romp on the grass.

Pam did not step on the crab.

Did Fran bump his leg?

Gram can get this spot off the mask.

2.2 B Sentences

we	for	go	her	she	he	or	are	you	do	Mr.

Tom will test the drums for the band.

Bev grins when she sits in the sun.

Fran sped up the hill in his hot rod.

The mast of the ship is up.

It is a thrill to win at chess.

It is just a hunch that I will win.

I think that Jan is a snob.

That man must get help.

Bob is fond of that pink shell.

Ben is stiff from the long swim.

Mr. Smith is gruff.

My staff did the best job!

The smog is bad!

Meg will limp up the steps.

It is just a small spot on the rug.

The ball hit Tom in the chest.

We must get film for this trip.

Jim had to drink a glass of mil<u>k</u>.

The land in the west is flat.

I must plan to mend this dress.

The hunt did not go past dus<u>k</u>.

Bill got a grip on the drum.

Jed did the job with zest.

The dog sniffs the fish in the dish.

The staff felt sad when Jim left.

Brad slugs the ball with the bat.

Jim will help the old man cross the path.

Ted sets traps when he hunts.

Will you press the dress for <u>K</u>im?

2.2 B Sentences (continued)

Mom will yell if I crack the glass.

It is swell to camp at the cliff.

Fran will get the things on this long list.

Mr. Chang will pass the test.

Gram had a red quilt for Bev.

Did the lint block the vent?

Beth is glad that Chet had a ring for her.

Can the kids help hunt for the lost bell?

Fran will to lend his drill to Ned.

The cast was glad to do the class skit.

The welts on my leg throb.

The gust of wind sent his hat to the path.

Get the specks of lint off this dress.

Do not sulk when you are glum.

Bill will get that stock fund.

Jim lends cash to Pam in a flash.

Ben had the rest of the fresh plum.

The tint in the glass will block the sun.

2.3 A-B Words

bold	bind	host	kind	wild
told	blind	find	child	mind
old	hold	cold	sold	find
most	colt	mold	post	jolt
mild	bolt	fold	grind	gold

2.3 A Sentences

The child is not in the shop.

Bob did not find the small colt.

Jim was kind to the old man.

Fred went to get a wild hog.

The dog sat on his hind legs to beg.

The chimp did not mind the cold.

Wind the top and it will spin.

Do not drop trash in the wild wind.

The bus spun and hit the post.

Bob had a bad cold.

2.3 B Sentences

Jim was in a bind with Tom.

Sid did not wish to hold the cash for the band.

Jim told Beth that he was cold.

Brad sold his best gold ring.

It was not mild on the gulf, it was cold!

Tom is bold with his dad.

Bill is the best host.

Bob sold the old mink for lots of cash.

The child went to get the bolt for his dad.

2.4 A Words

stung	blank	swing	stink	bring
skunk	sting	trunk	prank	blink
drink	shrink	Frank	drank	shrunk
blast	grunt	stump	crunch	drift
twist	crisp	draft	print	slant
trust	grump	blend	craft	slept
slump	stamp	stand	stunt	blimp
cramp	plump	plant	shrimp	squint
grand	crust	spend	crept	branch
brings	skunks	stings	trunks	pranks
blinks	drinks	grunts	stumps	drifts
blends	crafts	slumps	blimps	plants

2.4 B Words

flank	clang	flunk	cling	spank
prong	brink	clunk	fling	spunk
drunk	frank	clank	swung	sling
thrust	stomp	frump	blitz	swift
clasp	blunt	French	tramp	trend
flint	brunch	thrift	primp	drench
crust	brisk	trump	bland	grant
clamp	tract	flask	gland	skimp
brand	scant	glint	cleft	clench
smelt	clomp	clump	crest	stint
trench	crimp	shift	stench	

2.4 B Words (continued)

blanch	graft	brunt	scamp	scalp
clings	spanks	slings	clomps	flunks
clasps	thrusts	clumps	stunts	

2.4 Nonsense

brist	drast	twend	prast	stemp
drant	plont	trost	crent	plond
slont	frast	grimp	plend	brent
blomp	twint	squomp	thront	shrent
dramp	glont	frist	thrasp	squent
slomp	trant	twost	brinch	crosp
gremp	clusp	fland	grisp	flosk
slopt	trimp	pront	drinch	glant
flamp	bresk	slamp	gront	plomp
thropt	cranch			

2.4 A Sentences

	I	you	for	her	go

The skunk stinks!

I got a chill from that bad draft.

Peg swept the rug with the brush.

The shrimp is on the top shelf.

Tim slept in the tent.

I will print on the pad.

Bob felt his leg twist.

Stan had ten shrimp for lunch.

Brad will blend the milk with the egg.

Russ slept on the cot.

I had a cramp in my left leg.

We must stand to sing this song.

Ben will twist off that lid.

Stop to rest and get a drink.

The frost did not help the crops.

We must get a stamp to send this.

The stump is on the path.

The tot crept to her dad.

The blimp did not go fast at all.

The k̲ids sat on the big clump of grass.

Bill trusts his k̲ids with his cash.

Did the plants in the den get sun?

The big prank was a blast.

2.4 B Sentences

| her | do | be | he | have | they | for | you | about | out | see | Mr. |

The k̲ids can clinch this win.

That was a big blast of wind!

Beth pants when she runs to the crest of the hill.

Brad was ill and did not have spunk.

The band cranks it up when they jam.

I will get a dress at the thrift shop.

He did not get a hit in his slump.

Brad will help get the logs in the trench.

I am fond of that red print.

Bob spent all his cash.

Did Rich flinch when the ball hit his chest?

Dad had brunch with Mr. Chung.

The drift did not melt at all.

Beth is the French gal with Tim.

Jack had a clasp and a ring for Kim.

Ben went out for brunch.

It is just grand to see Bob.

Did the plant wilt from the draft?

Jim told the twins about his bad slump.

Glen will hold the flask.

That is the best brand in this shop.

The man slept on the cold steps.

Did Dad grunt when he lost?

Ken held six trump in his hand.

This trend will not last long.

Did Tom flunk his big French test?

Jed can be a grump!

Jan had a tract of land in the west.

Brad must not clench his fists.

Beth had a plump fig.

Ed did not trust the man with the cash.

Did Jim and Peg get the big grant?

Ben had to trust his big staff.

Tim felt the crunch in his shop.

Trends in dress do not last long.

2.5 A Words

| strap | splash | string | split | scrub |
| strong | strip | scrap | spring | |

2.5 B Words

scrod	strum	sprint	tempt	struck
strand	stress	sprig	strep	scram
splint	strut	scruff	scrip	scrag
sprat	scrim	sprang	strung	sprit
script				

2.5 Nonsense

scrid	strang	sprab	stren	scraff
strup	scrill	struz	sploss	strub
spret	sprom	screm	strag	sprox
strupt	scrand	sprund	splent	sprant
spland	strimp	scromp	strump	scrund
stropt	scrupt			

2.5 A Sentences

see   I

I think that I can split the logs.

I must squint in this spring sun.

Chad will jump with a big splash.

Fran still has to scrub the pots.

Jim lost the strap on his bag.

That stuff is just scrap.

Jim is strong from his job.

The pup had a strip of cloth.

What is that strong smell?

I will mend the strap on this dress.

If Ted jumps, the splash will be big.

Jim will plant crops in the spring.

The dog got the scrap from lunch.

I told the child to scrub the tub.

2.5 B Sentences

I	do	for	Mr.	you	see

You will see buds on that branch in the spring.

The kids will split up that job.

Sid will get the strand of string for the job.

I just strum on the drums for fun.

At six a.m., Tim sprints on the path.

We will get shrimp and scrod.

Jan has the script for the class skit.

Mr. Smith must scrimp to get lunch.

Jed had to get a splint on his leg.

This job has lots of stress.

Bob will help us strip that bench.

The strut held up the wall.

The fresh sprig was on the desk.

Mom will get the scrub brush.

Dad sprang up at the shrill yell.

I felt lots of stress from that big job.

"What Says?"

Consonant Phonemes

3.1 - 3.4

/b/ - b	/p/ - p	/d/ - d
/kw/ - qu	/f/ - f	/r/ - r
/g/ - g	/s/ - s	/h/ - h
/t/ - t	/j/ - j	/v/ - v
/k/ - c, k, ck	/w/ - w, wh	/l/ - l
/ks/ - x	/m/ - m	/y/ - y
/n/ - n	/z/ - z, s (sometimes as a suffix)	/ch/ - ch
/th/ - th	/sh/ - sh	/hw/ - wh

Vowel Phonemes

3.1 - 3.4

/ă/ - a	/ĕ/ - e	/ĭ/ - i
/ŏ/ - o	/ŭ/ - u, ə (unstressed syllable - advanced students)	

Additional Sounds

3.1 - 3.4

/òl/ - all	/ang/ - ang	/ank/ - ank
/am/ - am	/ing/ - ing	/ink/ - ink
/an/ - an	/ong/ - ong	/onk/ - onk
	/ung/ - ung	/unk/ - unk
/īld/ - ild	/ōld/ - old	/ōst/ - ost
/īnd/ - ind	/ōlt/ - olt	

sunfish   relish   cactus

upset	nutshell	hotrod	tomcat	sunfish
puffball	bathmat	uphill	hatbox	catfish
Batman	dishpan	shellfish	tenpin	suntan
tiptop	lapdog	sunlit	cobweb	pigpen
bathtub	sunset	sunbath	zigzag	catnip
bedbug	pinball	index	mascot	whiplash
unzip	edit	napkin	publish	goblin
picnic	cactus	combat	admit	submit
until	Justin	public	undid	nutmeg
album	misfit	humbug	polish	punish
relish	limit	Kevin	habit	topic
tonic	robin	solid	panic	finish
cabin	exit			

ə and e = /i/

wagon	Boston	denim	lemon	pollen
oxen	tonsil	falcon	seven	melon
Texas	salad	rocket	velvet	ticket
basket	helmet	magnet	bucket	locket
jacket	pocket	packet	racket	

+s

bathtubs	pigpens	rockets	cabins	sunsets
magnets	helmets	jackets	picnics	goblins
robins	cobwebs			

3.1 B Words

ashcan	onset	setup	legman	hotbed
gunship	gunshot	upshot	pitfall	shotgun
catnap	within	onrush	madcap	bedpan
laptop	hubcap	potshot	mishmash	vanquish
bellman	candid	hobnob	jonquil	campus
pipkin	sublet	chitchat	bandit	mantis
expel	kidnap	septic	rustic	Dublin
tactic	victim	litmus	publish	optic
poplin	cancan	pulpit	hectic	enrich
tidbit	dispel	quintet	magnum	until
peptic	unpeg	aspen	talcum	convex
pepsin	anvil	Calvin	sextet	pundit
ramrod	limpid	impel	aspic	mimic
vivid	fetish	rapid	valid	credit
medic	lavish	debit	timid	vomit
toxic	avid	vanish	tepid	toxin
relic	sonic	profit	livid	epic
comic	banish	frolic	famish	gamut
rabid	radish	exam	latin	ethnic
kinship				

/ə/

tendon	model	sultan	atlas	seldom
linen	havoc	custom	pivot	canvas
anthem	linden	bedlam	vandal	random
sandal	signal	novel	panel	chapel
bigot	lentil	tinsel		

3.1 B Words (continued)

e = /i/

comet	tablet	musket	hamlet	casket
goblet	gasket	rivet	socket	

+s

gaskets	hubcaps	bandits	pivots	mimics
epics	devils	models	pitfalls	signals
goblets	bigots	comics	toxins	victims

3.1 Nonsense

gospen	galnic	pinmus	rabcot	optil
napfin	popmeg	litship	besnet	velvin
casbit	ziglid	tipdex	findid	hobnum
bishbat	fampel	enset	shotlet	taltic
musfit	tuplet	azbim	quislet	famjan
nixib	comvig	dothbet	gushim	queblet
vamtish	fetneg	exvim		

3.1 A Sentences

do   by   into   for   about   he   she   be   come

Sid did not miss the sunset.

Ben had catnip for the tomcat.

Jim is upset about the loss.

Bob got a sunfish with his rod.

Dad will dust the cobweb in the den.

Did Bret get the shellfish from Mom?

The dog in the bathtub is a mess.

The kids went to rent the Batman flick.

Frank thinks that he will finish last.

The wild bobcat hid in the shed.

Beth did not get upset when she lost.

Jill had fun with the magnet.

Do not drop the album in the slush.

Fill the basket with shells.

Did Kim admit that she felt a chill?

Stan put the napkin on his lap.

Kevin did not get upset with Jill.

Jim went to get catnip for the tomcat.

Dad got a magnet for Malcom.

Glen lost his red wagon.

Jan will come as a goblin.

Kim has a brass helmet.

Did Bob get a suntan on his trip?

Ed went to the cabin by the pond.

Justin must dust the cobweb off the shelf.

Kim went to the shop to finish the job.

The child did not wish to get in the bathtub.

Bill fell but did not get upset.

Tom and Jan will go on a picnic.

The magnet is on the top shelf.

We sat on the cliff at sunset.

Do not step in the pigpen!

The big blast upset the pup.

The sunfish is in the bathtub.

Beth has a satin and silk dress.

her   for   go   Mrs.   Ms.   said   they   have   into   I   out   over   saw   you

I think that Jan will publish this script.

The French class will be held at the west campus.

Bob did jump at the gunshot.

Kevin met Jan at the club.

Did the class mimic Ms. Lestic?

Will you get the boss a napkin?

Bob went to get Beth in his red Mustang.

The press did not want to panic the public.

It was hectic in the mall.

Mrs. Chan must submit the plan to the boss.

They must publish the net profit.

Did Sanchez get his jacket?

Milton did not wish to have radish in his salad.

Jill lost the tablet in the grass.

Tom was candid with his boss.

Stan had chicken and a salad.

Bill will go into combat.

That septic tank did smell bad.

The bandit got the cash.

Meg did not get the nutmeg.

Beth had an old goblet.

The dog will sniff the tidbit.

Can you dump that ashcan in the trash?

Rich felt timid when he was with Pam.

Sam went over his credit limit.

We must not let the victim vanish.

It is such a thrill to publish this!

3.1 B Sentences (continued)

Bob had a bad tendon in his left leg.

We must cut the sapling on this path.

Rest at that rustic cabin.

We must find the septic tank.

The man will hunt with a shotgun.

Sanchez had to get a gas<u>k</u>et for his van.

Patrick will visit his mom in <u>D</u>ublin.

3.2 A Words

slingshot	fishpond	blindfold	himself	wingspan
sandblast	sandlot	milkman	insist	chipmunk
hundred	disrupt	dentist	spandex	clinic
plastic	gumdrop	contest	sandwich	children
nonstop	bobsled	handbag	sandbox	frantic
pump<u>k</u>in	splendid	seventh	insult	Alfred
pretzel	absent	<u>k</u>ingdom	problem	dragon
pilgrim	talent	trumpet	planet	triplet
cricket	<u>k</u>ingfish	chestnut	tantrum	grandslam
windmill	invent	humpback		

+s

dentists	gumdrops	planets	chipmunks	chestnuts
pilgrim	trumpets	blindfolds	slingshots	windmills
pump<u>k</u>ins	crickets	problems	bobsleds	

standoff	windswept	upswing	holdup	handstand
offhand	shoplift	stepchild	uplift	offprint
gangplank	handclasp	snapshot	stronghold	landfill
handcuff	dropcloth	flagship	sunlamp	sunspot
milkshed	gunsmith	standstill	uphold	backhand
grassland	smallpox	crosscut	handball	locksmith
drumstick	mankind	grandchild	flintlock	postscript
handspring	spendthrift	wildcat	lipstick	upland
offspring	goldsmith	topmost	strongbox	windfall
goldfinch	gasmask	kinsman	freshman	fragment
expand	drastic	skeptic	extend	dragnet
segment	bankrupt	spastic	implant	unrest
entrap	skinflint	infest	contempt	transplant
transmit	complex	Midwest	unbend	content
itself	consist	consult	intend	conquest
gastric	disgust	credit	slipshod	entrust
tinsmith	compost	untold	contrast	culprit
indent	inept	instep	conscript	blemish
extent	humdrum	static	mustang	oblong
blandish	advent	tropic	inland	inquest
hamstring	British	pigskin	transit	unsung
engulf	enrich	upend	convent	enchant
pigment	unstrung			

impend	figment	gambrel	minstrel	plankton
tendril	tranquil	emblem	nostril	solvent
brethren	modest	<u>k</u>indred	crumpet	spigot
droplet	sprocket	trinket	husband	bracket

+s

pigments	handcuffs	bankrupts	handclasps	disgusts
expands	dropcloths	handstands	enchants	contrasts
indents	tropics	sprockets	transmits	s<u>k</u>eptics
credits	snapshots			

3.2 Nonsense

shupnest	shiblent	chinfrob	frentlap	thibselt
trendid	enflont	clupnet	thipnest	instom
timplet	contimp	stroplim	extrib	vambith
admest				

3.2 A Sentences

go   have   he   into   Mr.   or

Alfred will win the next contest.

The twist contest was fun.

Get the pump<u>k</u>in in the shed.

That bat had a six-inch wingspan.

Ted will insist that he got the best fish.

Tim was upset when he lost the contest.

We will get the nonstop jet.

The big problem upset Jeff.

Sam was not absent from math class.

Nelson was in the sandwich shop.

The chestnut fell into the hot pot.

Abdel is in the next contest.

Dad insists that Ben naps on his bed.

Jim had a bobsled on the hill.

Bob will go to the dentist.

Mom insists that we finish the job.

Beth had a splendid red dress.

Tim had a red trumpet in band class.

Did Seth win the contest?

Jan lost her handbag in the mall.

Alfred has lots of talent.

3.2 B Sentences

about	for	go	he	or	so	wood	Mr.	Mrs.	me	we

I intend to shop for lunch.

This standstill will set us back.

Ben got the ax from his strongbox.

I will publish this when I finish the subplot.

Wong had plankton in his fish tank.

That is the problem in a nutshell.

His suntan is from a sunlamp.

We must consult with his dentist.

Beth is content to sit in the sun.

Jim felt the distrust of his boss.

Mr. Leptus will suspend Jack from the class.

The man left the shop in disgust.

My husband got me this velvet dress.

Jim has a bad hamstring pull.

The tot had a bad tantrum with his dad.

3.2 B Sentences (continued)

The cop had the handcuffs on the punk.

Ted must set a dropcloth on the rug.

This is such a humdrum job!

Beth had a lung transplant.

The windmill sat at the top of the hill.

I think this is the best snapshot.

Jim was content in the sun.

Kristen gets the credit for this job.

Mr. Kemp will invest in gold.

The contest will consist of ten segments.

It was a complex problem.

The cops had the culprit in handcuffs.

Jim intends to win the handball contest.

I will go bankrupt with this big tax!

The shop was held up by men with handguns.

Ted disrupts the French class.

I think the culprits got the last gumdrops.

3.3 A Words

conduct	subject	object	inspect	exact
contract	insect	contact	distract	expect

3.3 B Words

compact	impact	district	inflict	induct
suspect	instinct	abstract	distinct	neglect
convict	obstruct	convect	concoct	extract
conflict	prospect			

3.3 A Sentences

you   for   me   are   Mr.   Mrs.   p.m.

Kelton must contact his mom.

Mrs. Wilson plans to inspect the desks.

Math is the next subject.

Can you distract Mr. Griffin for me?

The bad conduct got Mom mad.

Did Sam find the exact pin?

Tom did not expect Liz until six p.m.

Lots of insects are in the sandbox.

3.3 B Sentences

you Mr. about for her so go we into I by my have

Get the lemon extract for this frosting.

The boss had a problem with the contract.

The conflict with Jill must end.

That red Mustang is compact.

Did the insects infest the trash can?

Mr. Chang will stop that conflict.

Bob will concoct the mix.

The vet had to inject the dog with a shot.

I think that Ed has distinct math skills.

We will go check on that land prospect.

The cops had the suspect in handcuffs.

My instinct tells me not to go.

That subject is abstract.

Did Pat intend to contact Glen?

I felt the impact from the crash.

This district has big plans.

Her grin is so distinct!

3.4 A Words

athletic	Wisconsin	establish	Atlantic	snapdragon
hobgoblin	basketball	penmanship	fantastic	misconduct
Thanksgiving	punishment	inhabit		

3.4 B Words

consistent	columnist	investment	discredit	discontent
Wilmington	volcanic	invalid	inhibit	insistent
dogmatic	calisthenic	consensus	existent	inconsistent
kinesthetic	astonish	Hopkinton	inhabit	anesthetic
disenchant	subindex	Atlantis	bombastic	magnetic
exotic	imprison	cosmetic	transatlantic	disinfect
intrinsic	intrepid	quintuplet	diminish	inexact
admonish				

3.4 A Sentences

I   we   my   give

I think that this sandwich is fantastic!

The dentist is from Wisconsin.

My penmanship is the best in the class.

The class can expect a punishment.

We will give thanks on Thanksgiving.

Benson had the best shot with the basketball.

The boss did not wish to discredit him.

We must get a consultant to help us fix this mess.

Calvin was discontent with his job.

Dad must be consistent with the <u>k</u>ids.

I think that Bob is the best columnist.

He will establish himself in Wisconsin.

Mom is frantic about the investment plans.

Glen went to the athletic contest.

Elvis did not sing in Wilmington.

That is a volcanic topic!

We must get a bid in for that subcontract.

His misconduct upset Mom and Dad.

3.5 A Words

rented	shrinking	folded	drilling	grunted
jumping	handed	standing	twisted	swinging
squinted	splashing	dusted	singing	hunted
talented	insisting	unlisted	expanding	publishing
finishing	sandblasted	insulted	punishing	invented
expected	distracting			

3.5 B Words

discontented	subcontracted	disgusted	enchanted	expanded
uninhibited	extended	invested	enlisted	implanted
grasping	sprinting	drafting	vanishing	extending
shifting	establishing	squinting	enriching	subcontracting
lavishing	consulting	conducting		

3.5 A Sentences

her   are

Brad disrupted the math class.

Jill is finishing her glass of milk.

Chan invented that rocket.

He dented his hot rod in the crash.

Mom is still thinking of her job.

Ken was standing with his hands in his pockets.

The kids are singing a <u>L</u>atin song.

The fishing trip was fantastic.

3.5 B Sentences

her

That uninhabited spot must be tranquil.

Rob will get the lung transplanted in Wisconsin.

The enlisted men must be in combat.

Jenson is extending his visit with his dad.

Peg consulted with the bank.

The man is disgusted with the lack of plans.

Jan is visiting her dad.

Glen conducted the band and it was a thrill.

"What Says?"

Consonant Phonemes

4.1 - 4.4

/b/ - b	/p/ - p	/d/ - d
/kw/ - qu	/f/ - f	/r/ - r
/g/ - g	/s/ - s	/h/ - h
/t/ - t	/j/ - j	/v/ - v
/k/ - c, k, ck	/w/ - w, wh	/l/ - l
/ks/ - x	/m/ - m	/y/ - y
/n/ - n	/z/ - z, s (sometimes as a suffix or between 2 vowels)	
/ch/ - ch	/sh/ - sh	/th/ - th
/hw/ - wh		

Vowel Phonemes

4.1 - 4.4

/ă/ - a	/ā/ - **a-e**	/ĕ/ - e
/ē/ - **e-e**	/ĭ/ - i	/ī/ - **i-e**
/ŏ/ - o	/ō/ - **o-e**	
/ŭ/ - u, ə (unstressed syllable-advanced students)		
/ū/ - **u-e**	/ü/ - **u-e**	

Additional Sounds

4.1 - 4.4

/ȯl/ - all	/ang/ - ang	/ank/ - ank
/am/ - am	/ing/ - ing	/ink/ - ink
/an/ - an	/ong/ - ong	/onk/ - onk
	/ung/ - ung	/unk/ - unk
/īld/ - ild	/ōld/ - old	/ōst/ - ost
/īnd/ - ind	/ōlt/ - olt	

4.1 A Words

lime	ape	tide	these	cube
<u>wh</u>ine	lane	wide	cake	line
pole	flame	hose	nine	vase
tube	those	chase	spine	dare
grade	case	vote	file	care
mile	came	bone	cone	wife
smile	note	choke	dime	drive
mine	flute	tape	share	joke
chose	wave	hide	name	pile
close	bite	hope	wine	slope
ride	plane	poke	rule	plate
rise	scrape	throne	spoke	lake
prize	rope	s<u>k</u>ate	cave	dive
snake	shine	hole	cane	quake
tune	slide	trade	fire	<u>wh</u>ale
prune	<u>wh</u>ite	bake	like	grape
ripe	globe	mule	<u>k</u>ite	wipe
state	home	sale	bike	shake
stone	save	maze	shave	bride
take	strike	base	time	brave
shape	Dave	Steve	Mike	<u>K</u>ate
Jane	Pete	Jake	Duke	James
June	safe	broke	hate	five
game	life	rake	late	

+s

plates	ropes	games	stripes	whales
rules	rakes	globes	mazes	slides
likes	jokes	grades	votes	tides
whines	flames	cares	bones	cases
shares	scrapes	hides	planes	waves
trades	dives	slopes	grapes	prunes

4.1 B Words

quite	date	hire	code	daze
fake	hate	rude	slave	zone
prone	blaze	robe	scale	crave
drape	scrape	sane	mole	fade
stole	mute	sake	drone	dupe
glaze	grope	glare	pane	slate
stare	pride	shame	quote	haze
spade	chime	craze	dine	stale
clothe	stake	snipe	spike	thrive
rote	spare	swipe	flake	tote
gripe	scare	blare	yoke	flare
tone	bathe	blade	Blake	braze
stride	lobe	rite	lame	strobe
spite	dare	chafe	brute	lathe
trite	crude	hare	prune	fare
tithe	rare	fife	bare	mime
cove	gale	spire	e<u>ke</u>	dose
chive				

4.1 B Words (continued)

lone	theme	nude	jive	yoke
twine	dune	rove	vane	cure
brine	mate	pure	hone	jade
mope	rave	pike	blame	tribe
spade	rife	drone	rate	spike
probe	shrine	doze	slate	<u>wh</u>ile
lame	slime			

+s

strikes	snores	hopes	flakes	gropes
states	zones	dines	strokes	hides
quakes	stores	panes	sites	codes
dupes	chokes	fakes	rites	craves
scales	dives	times	hates	hires
gripes	scones	pokes	glares	trades

4.1 Nonsense

vime	quipe	jire	bope	draze
frope	gake	nole	fline	grude
wose	slive	bine	flome	jope
smule	hape	prane	fote	glute
blate	chope	kine	dreve	scobe
dafe	scole	wime	creve	spive
stine	frote			

I   for   she   have   go   we   they   be   down   you   your   my   by   do   he   her   into   me   Mr.
out   our   p.m.   their   since

I like the tune that <u>K</u>ate will sing.

I left the bone on my plate.

Is it safe to ride my bike on that path?

I will trade this packet of gum.

The wise <u>k</u>ing sat on his throne.

I had the best grade in math class.

I think there is a snake in that hole.

Ed broke the rules.

Dave was late for the dentist.

I hope I have a packet of gum.

Dad told a joke that made us all smile.

Get the tickets for the bas<u>k</u>etball game.

Sid has a flute to bring to band class.

Beth likes her pink and white pants.

Hank has a limp and must use a cane.

Did the pup choke on that bone?

Mrs. Smith has the best smile.

Dad will drive the <u>k</u>ids to class.

We will slide and then go skate.

James will take the flag off the pole.

That humpback whale was big!

Mike invented a game with lots of rules.

Calvin will finish the quiz in time for lunch.

I will ride my fine bike.

Go to the cave next to the lake.

The bride had a fine time.

Jane must save to get that dress.

The sun shines on the pond.

If you win the game, you will get a prize.

After we skate, we will go home.

James dove into the cold pond.

We can slide on that hill slope.

That blast made us all jump.

The plane will cross the Atlantic.

We will shake and bake the chicken.

We will make a cake with frosting and gumdrops.

The rules in this class are quite strict.

The plum is ripe but the grapes are bad.

I like to stroke my cat.

My dad has to shave and dress.

In June, we can swim in the lake.

Did Mom ask me to shake the rug?

Dad likes to save all this old junk.

Did Steve drop chestnuts in that hole?

Wipe up the mess and get the plates for lunch.

Kate will get the shrimp on sale.

It will take a long time to wipe up this mess.

Mike got the prize at the end of the contest.

Dave cuts the grass and then Alfred rakes.

Ken slid into home plate to win.

Spike, the cat, had a plate of fish.

The sun shines on that cactus plant.

James did not have a spare tire.

I hope to make a trade-in for this old van.

Pete fell off the rise of the big wave.

This ham sandwich is stale.

Dale insisted that we sit in the shade.

The stale smoke in the club made me ill.

We will share the bid to close the contract.

Jane got the red linen dress on sale.

Kate ate the cake with milk.

Jim hit a grandslam in the game.

That insult was rude.

Kevin likes to dare Ed.

Mr. Jones held the ten of spades.

Steve has a snapshot of a white whale.

Bill intends to shave and dress for the banquet.

Glen sat by the fire.

I suspect that the shop will close at nine.

Pete intended to get a spare tire for his van.

Mr. Jones must hire a consultant.

It is a shame that Kate lost her handbag.

Pete hopes to go on a date with Jan.

James was quite glad to go home.

Ed will stoke up the fire.

The man plans to shake my hand.

Pete drove into the pole and got whiplash.

I will be late for the basketball game.

It is a shame that Mr. Lang went bankrupt.

I will jog in spite of the cold.

Jane is singing that tune.

I like the jazz of Duke Ellington.

I hope to hire Bob Swift.

I like to gaze at the sunsets in Texas.

I crave hot chi<u>ck</u>en salad for lunch.

Our mascot will miss the big game.

We will dine at home this eve.

The freshman class did not like the strict rules.

Mrs. Ross has lots of pride in her children.

Can you tell me the name of that fish?

The tame mule will take our bags up the cliff.

Jane likes limes.

Mr. Jones will get the bus at nine.

Beth likes to quote her dad.

Jake did not have a dime left to his name.

The columnist got a quote from Calvin.

Willis had the stakes for the tent in his van.

Pat saves all his cash.

The flames of the fire extended up the wall.

James will not share his bad jokes with us.

Dave cuts the grass and then Dale rakes.

Justin likes his distinct role at the bank.

4.2 A Words

campfire	flagpole	rosebud	handshake	kingsize
classmate	baseball	springtime	mil_k_shake	clambake
sunstroke	gatepost	grapevine	caveman	fishplate
inside	lifetime	fishline	firemen	manhole
sunrise	admire	dictate	unsafe	trombone
volume	invite	bedtime	inhale	costume
basement	lifelong	frustrate	fireball	escape
confuse	dislike	concrete	exhale	postpone
umpire	mistake	entire	software	vampire
stampede	advise	compete	inflate	homemade
athlete	explode	include	tadpole	complete
reptile	pancake	whalebone	spareribs	wildlife
frostbite	cupcake	handmade	landslide	pinhole
baseline	childlike	ringside	stovepipe	compare
clockwise	homesick	hemline	hotcake	statement
bagpipe				

4.2 B Words

nameplate	cashmere	flashcube	upgrade	franchise
bobwhite	spitfire	wineglass	sidestep	backstroke
filtrate	fireside	crossfire	namesake	sidewise
windpipe	snaredrum	sidetrack	crossbones	homeland
whitecap	landscape	grindstone	whitewall	postdate
flagstone	firetrap	nosedive	ragtime	telltale
limestone	sidelong	update	fanfare	primrose
wildfire				

4.2 B Words (continued)

millstone	sideswipe	offside	shipshape	sulfate
makeshift	pipestem	wineskin	sunbathe	pileup
stoneware	slantwise	firebox	oldline	mundane
exclude	inflame	compose	estate	aspire
impure	pulsate	decade	expose	hostile
impale	ignite	subside	lactose	encase
capsize	gangrene	mandate	octane	translate
methane	intrude	midwife	condone	transpire
cascade	shipmate	convene	insane	fixate
invoke	incline	console	disrobe	flatware
inmate	subscribe	filtrate	welfare	bonfire
enclose	yuletide	engrave	extreme	unclothe
inquire	confide	contrive	obscure	upscale
inscribe	transpose	membrane	ingrate	contrite
compile	excrete	dispute	enthrone	adhere
impede	lignite	concave	magnate	obtuse
disclose	baptize	alcove	oxide	encode
uptake	firebug	milestone	sideslip	brimstone
lactate				

4.2 Nonsense

capsate	vilmite	trenzime	dispote	transdope
exbale	conbrile	endame	filkipe	explobe
drenzime	disfume	doselit	plebmat	glibmax
fretjome	laxtile	oppreve	drenvile	mentrabe
colgrone	pulvene	lebetrom	rettume	

WRS DICTATION BOOK | STEPS 1-6   **63**

Mr. Lane went inside the damp cave.

Dave will get a trombone in June.

Eve has a strong handshake!

It is unsafe to cross that path.

The class reptile is lost in the lab.

Kate will complete the job.

The red rug is in the basement.

It was a mistake to ignore him.

Did Ben vote for his classmates?

I like to sit by the campfire and sing songs.

My classmate got the top prize.

I think I will invite Zeke.

Ed had pancakes and ham at brunch.

I like the springtime best.

My milk and cupcake did not last long.

This problem does frustrate me!

Steve and Tom sat by the fireside.

The children were upset when it was bedtime.

The class will dislike this math problem.

Steve had spareribs and a salad.

That software will cost us lots of cash.

Dad gave Jim a fine handshake.

Eve will go to the sandlot baseball game.

Dave Smith will be the umpire for the second game.

We must escape from this damp cave.

I had a cupcake and milk.

Did you drop this note on the pavement?

4.2 A Sentences (continued)

I think that Jane is a fine athlete.

Pete and Jake will compete in the contest.

I do not like to make a mistake.

It is bad to inhale the smoke.

The wire is in the basement.

Did you dislike that joke?

We must drive to the shop to rent a costume.

Dave will inflate the raft and take it on the lake.

4.2 B Sentences

you	for	during	have	we	her	Mr.	about	my	under	your	

Can you compute those math problems?

The volume of sales went up!

Ben objects to the entire plan.

I think that <u>K</u>en will invite Jane to the prom.

The consultant must advise the staff.

That old shed is such a firetrap.

The console TV will fit in the den.

Dave fell on the flagstone and had to go to the clinic.

The boss gave a mandate to her staff.

I will inquire about the baseball game.

Use the best octane gas when you fill the tank in my truck.

The infant can not have the lactose in milk.

I hate this extreme cold!

Mr. Jones was the umpire for the entire game.

Compare this prospect with the other investments.

Did the wind subside at last?

Ignite a flame for the stove.

We must get an update from James.

Kate made a big mistake on her taxes.

The staff had to compile the list of old investments.

Mr. Chase gave a statement to the press.

Ethel put on makeup and lipstick.

The landscape here is fantastic!

We made a big bonfire for the clambake.

Ben had whitewall tires on his red Mustang.

Mr. Miles intended to sit at ringside.

The contract dispute ended at last.

The gong in the camp rang at sunrise.

The old man in this snapshot is your namesake.

That ragtime tune made me smile.

It was a mistake to get that software.

Mike will pin up the hemline on those pants.

The men intend to invade the tribe.

Dad did not let the kids intrude on his game.

Did the stove explode to make such a blast?

It is a shame that you did not invite Steve.

The van fell into the pothole and got a flat tire.

We will get more concrete to finish the job.

Mrs. Flome will win the vote by a landslide.

I confide in my wife when I have a problem.

Did that van sideswipe my Mustang?

4.3 A Words

postponement	recognize	distribute	tranquilize	valentine
contribute	demonstrate	incomplete		

4.3 B Words

administrate	infantile	contribute	demonstrate	infiltrate
contemplate	disenfranchise	inundate	monoxide	enfranchise
compensate	victimize	confiscate	indispose	

4.3 A Sentences

about   we   you

The vet must tranquilize the pup with a shot.

James must demonstrate the math problem.

Kate was upset about the postponement of the game.

The costume is still incomplete.

We will contribute to the class fund.

Jake will help distribute the notes to the class.

Can you demonstrate that handshake?

I think Steve gave Robin a big valentine.

4.3 B Sentences

for   after   Mr.   Ms.

The cops will confiscate that cash.

Sheldon will administrate the west campus.

We must find a consultant to help with the script.

The plans for this district are still incomplete.

His infantile statement did not escape the press.

I like to contribute to that fund.

We did not recognize the truck after the crash.

That monoxide gas made me sick.

The boss was upset that the job was still incomplete.

His stunt was infantile.

We must compensate for this loss in cash.

Ken must contemplate that problem.

Mr. Yang will distribute the checks.

Mrs. Sanchez plans to compensate her staff well.

4.4 A-B Words

give	live	olive	active	have
captive	disruptive	impulsive	expensive	inactive
inexpensive				

4.4 B Words

inflective	compulsive	intensive	subjective	constructive
expansive	inductive	distinctive	extensive	

4.4 A Sentences

we   my   for   I

The tot was active on the plane.

We live in Texas but Gabe lives in Kansas.

That shrimp salad sandwich is expensive.

Seth will give his dog a big hug.

Cliff did not like the black olive.

The kids held the pup captive for a joke.

That kid in my class is quite disruptive.

Fred is just a bit impulsive.

I hope the red silk dress is inexpensive.

Steve did not think the help was constructive.

The expansive land in Wisconsin is a wise investment.

We can get that expensive console TV.

We must invest in extensive software.

Beth tends to be a bit compulsive.

Mr. Jones will get extensive help from Malcom.

It is instinctive for my well-bred dog to hunt.

Kate met the topmost objective for the club.

The bus trip to Kansas is quite expensive.

The intensive contest lasted a long time.

"What Says?"

Consonant Phonemes

5.1 - 5.5

/b/ - b	/p/ - p	/d/ - d
/kw/ - qu	/f/ - f	/r/ - r
/g/ - g	/s/ - s	/h/ - h
/t/ - t	/j/ - j	/v/ - v
/k/ - c, k, ck	/w/ - w, wh	/l/ - l
/ks/ - x	/m/ - m	/y/ - y
/n/ - n	/z/ - z, s (sometimes as a suffix or between 2 vowels)	
/ch/ - ch	/th/ - th	/sh/ - sh
/hw/ - wh		

Vowel Phonemes

5.1 - 5.2

/ă/ - a	/ā/ - a-e, **a** (open syllable)	/ĕ/ - e
/ē/ - e-e, **e** (open syllable)	/ĭ/ - i	/ī/ - i-e, **i** (open syllable), **y** (first or only open syllable)
/ŏ/ - o	/ō/ - o-e, **o** (open syllable)	/ŭ/ - u
/ū/ - u-e, **u** (open syllable)	/ü/ - u-e, **u** (open syllable)	

5.3

/ē/ - e-e, **e** (open syllable), **y** (open syllable at end of a multisyllabic word)

5.5

/ŭ/ - u, ə (a and i in unstressed open syllables)

Additional Sounds

5.1 - 5.5

/ȯl/ - all	/ang/ - ang	/ank/ - ank
/am/ - am	/ing/ - ing	/ink/ - ink
/an/ - an	/ong/ - ong	/onk/ - onk
	/ung/ - ung	/unk/ - unk
/īld/ - ild	/ōld/ - old	/ōst/ - ost
/īnd/ - ind	/ōlt/ - olt	

5.1 A Words

cry	flu	ho	hi	sky
so	shy	me	we	fry
by	no	try	go	my
fly	I	he	she	why

5.1 B Words

pro	ply	be	spry	sly
ye	sty	pi	lo	pry

5.1 Nonsense

tro	plu	re	che	clo
sple	sle	cha	spo	bro
ste	plo	spu	twy	cle
dro	spro	bre	stru	de
mo	cly	po	za	stry
bu	tha	spru	scra	cre
fru				

5.1 A Sentences

Mom will fry the bass.

My Gram will fly to Wisconsin.

We expect to go home.

The firemen will try to use the hose on the fire.

We can make pancakes with Dad.

I have no costume yet.

Did she cry at bedtime?

We had a splendid time at the game.

Go inspect that nest of ants.

I think that he is shy with Kate.

I wish that Tom would be less impulsive.

My husband is a golf pro at that club.

Dave has the flu so he will not go to the game.

Jake will cry if he lost that belt.

I think that the salesman was quite sly.

The impact will not be so bad.

Can you try to pry this lid off?

5.2 A Words

behind	beside	label	human	pretend
remind	rewind	zero	erupt	begin
protest	silent	demand	behave	tulip
student	skyline	unite	motel	prevent
pupil	retire	banjo	rodent	locate
frozen	ozone	remote	robot	began
minus	siren	moment	depend	polite
request	beware	prepare	female	define
open	rotate	silo	humid	protect
rerun	even	donate	myself	frequent
bonus	refund	menu	program	migrate
respect	secret	respond	reflex	declare
defrost	recline	predict	basic	hotel
Irish	relax	result	defend	eject

frozen	decode	hybrid	resale	relate
prolong	mucus	event	canine	divest
focus	native	propel	repent	profane
Cupid	cubic	revere	crisis	feline
require	revive	profile	decal	repel
sequel	omit	lotus	bypass	basin
raven	deduct	reject	climax	item
trisect	Polish	tripod	basis	defect
elope	denote	vacate	detach	erect
erase	devote	stipend	erupt	mutate
sinus	revise	rebate	provide	python
unit	potent	proton	dilate	equate
detest	haven	dilute	stupid	zenith
duplex	edict	debate	bisect	apex
elate	refine	relent	promote	revoke
depict	amen	beheld	bequest	bison
befit	blatant	beget	beset	brazen
crusade	cremate	crocus	cubit	debase
defile	deject	delete	delude	demise
demure	demon	derive	desire	devise
elect	emit	equip	evil	evoke
haven	humane	lupine	locus	obese
prefab	preside	preset	presume	pagan
primate	probate	procure	profuse	prudent
radon	rebuke	refuse	refute	remake
remit				

resist	reset	reside	resume	retake
rotund	sedan	biplane	deprive	hatred
vibrate	refresh	deplete	restrict	deflect
preshrunk	regret	despite	decline	refract
nylon	replete	restore	putrid	declare
deflate	deprave	detract	fragrant	matrix
bronco	solo	banjo	veto	halo
gusto	tempo	limbo	bingo	migrant
microbe	macron	preclude	sacrum	vagrant
senile	hydrate	strident	vacant	

ə

final	legal	brutal	focal	fatal
rival	vital	vocal	local	oval
total	natal	tribal	frugal	papal
profit				

5.2 Nonsense

restrimp	prestope	trymest	trumepe	ploshent
streblent	ploton	frolipe	glosop	prespere
brytome	crozump	blenet	rebelt	protrum
triglone	tridem	flothine	grystod	delum
reflimp				

your   our   you

The student did not relax.

You must protect your skin in the sun.

Ms. Smith was quite polite when she spoke.

We must request a refund on this dress.

Jim was silent when he got the prize.

Tim must deflate the raft.

I will relax at the lake with Jason and David.

We will spend some time at the motel.

I admit that I like this program.

The lake is frozen, so we can skate.

We did not locate the lost ball.

I predict that our class will win.

Did the students behave?

I hope that cat can take care of the rodents.

Bruno has a secret to tell Fran.

The class was silent when Mr. Salvo visited.

In a moment, I will tell you the joke.

We will plant tulips with Bill.

That stone home is still vacant.

This student is quite polite in class.

Robin likes that fragrant smell.

It is human to make a mistake.

A pupil from Ohio will visit this class.

The Irish jig is lots of fun.

Eject that videotape.

women   could   you   need   for   day   about   Mr.   Dr.   they   pay

Kent regrets spilling his drink on the rug.

Jim had a wild decal on his pink van.

We will prepare to go on strike.

The last program is about to begin.

He must deduct that item from the bill.

We will check-in at the hotel and then go dine.

The boss prevented the dispute at the shop.

I wish we could escape from this humid day.

Bob will donate cash to the Crisis Fund.

Mike has a fine duplex in Boston.

That student is in Poland on a trip.

We prevented problems with this contract.

I regret that Jeff will not make the event.

Rod will have to defend his plan.

My dad went to demand a refund.

The staff can provide you with help.

Bill plans to retire and devote time to the project.

I regret the last class vote.

Can you donate to this program?

My Spanish class elected to take the final exam.

I will escape to the hotel to relax.

Did Jason deflate the raft?

We have to repel these insects!

I will inquire about the crisis.

I demand that you locate the missing file.

A dog is a canine and a cat is a feline.

Bev will refuse the gift from Chad.

The mob is yelling in protest.

You can begin the objective test.

I hope that they do not destruct the old mill.

We are depending on Jim to save the club.

Dr. Jones will prescribe a pill for my flu.

He plans to secure the vacant lot.

Ed is a migrant from Scotland.

Ted Mason has a strong desire to win.

Mr. Chang is protesting the strike.

Jim likes to pretend that he is rich.

We will restrict the time that you spend at the club.

Sheldon did not respond to my note.

Why did Jane refuse to wipe the tripod?

You must declare the profit and pay the tax.

5.3 A Words

jelly	puppy	funny	belly	buggy
lady	jolly	dizzy	plenty	happy
fifty	silly	handy	ruby	baby
penny	daddy	empty	granny	nasty
trolly	sunny	skinny	cozy	duty
angry	crazy	candy	pony	navy
pantry	lobby	tidy	holly	ivy
taffy	puny	pansy	gravy	

lazy	tiny	bunny	Tammy	Billy
Timmy	Jimmy	Wendy	Tony	Cathy
Toby	Amy	Sally	Molly	Sandy
Henry	Eddy			

5.3 B Words

sissy	belfry	giddy	crony	folly
canny	envy	musty	shinny	shanty
eddy	zany	dandy	nifty	sultry
cranny	sentry	cranky	rally	entry
daffy	petty	caddy	filly	holy

5.3 A Sentences

her   for

I dislike this lumpy gravy.

Dad will take Sandy to the ranch for a pony ride.

That old man is so jolly!

The entire cabin is filthy.

Betty is such a silly kid.

Dad demands that I empty this trash can.

The baby got a tan on her belly.

Wendy was selfish with the candy.

Get the chestnuts in the pantry.

Jim must provide us with a copy of his plans.

We will ride the trolly to the mall.

That student has plenty of talent.

James is quite handy at the shop.

My daddy will bring home a puppy.

Tommy had plenty of cash for the big event.

That crazy kid did not behave.

Did Sally get dizzy from her flu shot?

Jimmy dislikes jelly in his donuts.

The baby was so tiny when she came home.

This ivy plant will do well in that spot.

5.3 B Sentences

	Mr.	their	do	they	saw

Billy will caddy at that golf club.

Bobby and Jenny like to save nifty things.

What is that nasty smell in the pantry?

Did Molly get that expensive ruby?

The press felt it was their duty to publish all the facts.

Mr. Jones got quite angry with his staff.

I think that Sally can be nasty.

Mr. Smith will retire at sixty-five.

Jim felt his envy rise when he saw Jane with Stan.

It is musty in that old cabin.

Molly was so cranky at the shop.

Jimmy will enlist in the navy.

Dolly is lazy and has not done the job yet.

I do not to trust that lady at all.

The debate will be held in the lobby of the hotel.

I think that Mr. Chilty is happy with this plan.

James intends to tidy the shop and go home.

This job will be complete in plenty of time.

The students in the lobby are quite giddy.

5.4 A Words

cons<u>on</u>ant	melody	galaxy	comprehend	develop
elastic	microscope	disrespect	regulate	impolite
enemy	demolish	tuxedo	coconut	volcano

5.4 B Words

educate	absolute	hydroplane	rejuvenate	obsolete
electron	delinquent	isolate	human<u>k</u>ind	stipulate
cohesive	invasive	evaluate	microscopic	romantic
represent	remodel	responsive	repulsive	economy
colonist	economize	diplomat	defensive	hemoglobin
electrode	retrospect	insulin	tabulate	stimulate
faculty	incubate	egotist	dioxide	strangulate
utensil	monopolize	humanistic	humanize	monotone
patronize	amputate	speculate	prolific	imprudent
exodus	balcony	alfresco	document	amnesty
ebony	relinquish	agony	condensate	indolent
eloquent	redundant	dependent	pendulum	confiscate
adhesive	exclusive	explosive	economic	impudent
intrusive	inclusive	populate	monotony	renovate
obtrusive	pantomime	simulate	protrusive	retrofit
replenish	monogram	agonize	prohibit	antagonize
reflexive	reflective	industry	retrograde	equivocate
deregulate	infantry			

James likes to sing that melody to the baby.

Wendy will find all the consonants on this list.

The galaxy is so much fun to study.

enry must rent a tuxedo for the prom.

This elastic will hold the lid on the box.

We can see this small object with a microscope.

Amy plans to develop her talent on skates.

We must develop a skit for the class.

It is impolite to stare.

Bill likes to munch on coconut candy.

5.4 B Sentences

Mr.   they   read   for   would   over   goes   too   could   her   out   been   you   about

Mr. Strom must not violate his contract.

I think that reptile is repulsive.

Jimmy will evaluate the plan.

Betsy likes to monopolize the class.

This faculty represents the best in the state.

That man spoke in a monotone.

We must develop a plan to remodel this home.

This is a romantic spot.

Tommy had an explosive protest.

I think this product is obsolete.

The economy is still strong.

Did James win the all-inclusive trip?

We must renovate the old shed.

I must pass this math class to graduate.

Jenny was impolite to her dad in the lobby of the hotel.

Itemize the bill and send them a copy.

They plan to regulate the cost of gas.

Jake represented Tom for the big case.

Pete rented a tuxedo to go to the prom.

The elastic held the lid on the jug.

Hire a consultant to evaluate this program.

Jimmy will calculate the math problems.

The kids did not demolish the script

We will isolate Tommy from the class.

A fantastic video club will open in the spring.

Ken is in agony over his loss.

I would like to rejuvenate that old mill.

Did the salesman have this novelty item?

Mr. Henry hopes to stimulate the project.

James is such a diplomat.

Must we incubate these ostrich eggs?

A humanistic welfare program will help.

The economy in this state is not bad.

The faculty will have a banquet.

The document was lost in the trash.

Mr. Fresno likes to speculate with stocks.

Rod and his date will dine alfresco.

This skyline balcony is so fantastic!

If you isolate my pup, she will be sad.

We must care for this planet that we populate.

Stan has the exclusive copy of the script.

Adhesive tape can do the job well.

5.5 A Words

a

arise	extra	delta	abandon	Atlanta
Sandra	awaken	awhile	alone	alive
awoke	amaze	Alaska	aside	amuse

i

substitute	confident	hesitate	apricot	domino
compliment	continent	gravity	cabinet	cavity
animal	president	investigate	festival	

5.5 B Words

a

stigma	ultra	tundra	toga	vista
stanza	dogma	Kenya	alfalfa	fibula
quota	scuba	gala	rotunda	yoga
atomic	abuse	adapt	amid	aloft
acute	anemic	abide	agaze	abode
atone	abolish	aline	adept	manipulate
kabob	manila			

i

sensitive	stabilize	estimate	subsidize	subsidy
indirect	platitude	fumigate	platinum	mutilate
scrutinize	lubricate	manicure	halibut	subdivide
duplicate	instigate	silicone	implicate	sanitize
nominate	minimize	optimum	mobilize	medicate
imitate	dominate	litigate	sentiment	antiquate
abstinent	maximize	altitude	antidote	cultivate
complicate	indicate	denigrate	oxidize	magnitude
obligate	dignity	candidate	ventilate	fabricate
detriment	amplitude	entity	condiment	palpitate
culminate	destiny	meditate	radical	primitive
chastity	indigo	vanity	denizen	sentinel

5.5 B Words (continued)

i

manifold	resident	multitude	episode	activate
dedicate	epidemic	emigrate	evident	comical
optimize	habitat	brevity	liquidate	liniment
optimist	penitent	plenitude	politics	practical
punitive	reprimand	rudiment	ruminate	utilize
validate	vindicate	dividend	minimum	institute
captivate	ridicule	confidant	criminal	optimistic
discriminate	contaminate	amenity	intoxicate	consolidate
invalidate	eliminate	aluminum	humility	insensitive
intoxicant	utility			

5.5 A Sentences

you   does   her

a

The state of Alaska has lots of frozen tundra.

The baby awoke and began to cry.

Did that trick amaze the class?

The club will fly on a Delta jet to Atlanta.

Timmy insists that he will have extra time.

His instinct did amaze me.

Sandra does not like to be alone at all.

i

Rosa is the class president.

We must not hesitate.

The dentist must drill my cavity.

Get the domino set on the top shelf.

Eva likes all the animals in the pet shop.

We have had a substitute in class.

Can you name the seven continents?

Sandra had to go to the hospital.

That cabinet is a mess!

Mrs.   Mr.   for   you   our   your   into   her

a

Sandra must submit the script to Mr. K̲imes.

Sally will complete the last stanza of her song.

Sandy will discuss the trip to K̲enya at the club.

Tammy likes to add alfalfa to her salad.

The boss was glad that we made the sales quota.

Mr. Lang insisted that we abide by the rules.

The academy students will compete in the contest.

Tony will go for a scuba dive on his trip.

Edna will invite Tom to the gala event.

We will abandon that product line.

I must adapt to the class rules.

An unexpected problem arose.

With the conflict aside, Jim will begin the task.

Take care not to awa̲k̲en the children.

The boss hopes to duplicate the sales.

i

We must ventilate the basement.

Mr. Banty is such an optimistic man.

Dave gave Sandra a compliment that made her blush.

The democratic candidate will visit this school.

This will complicate the mess even more!

I hope we can ventilate the shed.

Beth has sensitive skin.

Did Tommy nominate you for class president?

Glen plans to go to that institute for welding.

Did the baby try to imitate Jimmy?

The salesman will estimate the cost.

Did Sandra spend the cash for a manicure?

Lenny did not instigate the conflict.

Grandma will use an old antidote.

Did he indicate the problem?

The class likes to debate politics.

The magnitude of the problem is evident.

That gas will contaminate the pond.

We must utilize all of our help.

Lakesha did a comical act for the class.

Mrs. Sanchez plans to eliminate that program.

I hope this flu is not an epidemic.

Drop the aluminum cans into the bin.

You must not discriminate.

Can you dedicate this next song to Sandy?

I think that episode is a rerun.

---

i

Validate your ticket at a shop in the mall.

Mike Rosa is an optimistic man.

Mrs. Costanza will reprimand the child.

That prank is quite a practical joke.

The residents were upset with the tax.

The apricot jam is on the shelf in the pantry.

"What Says?"

Consonant Phonemes

6.1 - 6.4

/b/ - b	/p/ - p	/d/ - d
/kw/ - qu	/f/ - f	/r/ - r
/g/ - g	/s/ - s	/h/ - h
/t/ - t	/j/ - j	/v/ - v
/k/ - c, k, ck	/w/ - w, wh	/l/ - l
/ks/ - x	/m/ - m	/y/ - y
/n/ - n	/z/ - z, s (sometimes as a suffix or between 2 vowels)	
/ch/ - ch	/sh/ - sh	/th/ - th
/hw/ - wh		

6.2 - 6.4

/d/ - d, **-ed**	/t/ - t, **-ed**

Vowel Phonemes

6.1 - 6.4

/ă/ - a	/ā/ - a-e, a (open syllable)	
/ĕ/ - e	/ē/ - e-e, e (open syllable), y (open syllable at end of a multisyllabic word)	
/ĭ/ - i	/ī/ - i-e, i (open syllable), y (first and only open syllable)	
/ŏ/ - o	/ō/ - o-e, o (open syllable)	
/ŭ/ - u, ə	/ū/ - u-e, u (open syllable)	/ü/ - u-e, u (open syllable)

Additional Sounds

6.1 - 6.4

/ȯl/ - all	/ang/ - ang	/ank/ - ank
/am/ - am	/ing/ - ing	/ink/ - ink
/an/ - an	/ong/ - ong	/onk/ - onk
	/ung/ - ung	/unk/ - unk
/īld/ - ild	/ōld/ - old	/ōst/ - ost
/īnd/ - ind	/ōlt/ - olt	

6.1 Suffixes

en	ness	ful	ment	ly
er	ish	ive	ty	est
es	less	able	y	

6.1 A Words

selfish	dependable	grumpy	babyish	protective
quicken	secretly	lonely	brushes	refreshment
shipment	pinkish	kindness	handful	freshen
gruffness	lucky	fluffy	kindly	plateful
frequently	respectful	equipment	hanger	taxes
splashes	stronger	disrespectful	strongest	amusement
refundable	longest	hopeless	lately	singer
wishes	strongly	wildest	lunches	safety
active	trustful	shyness	faster	fastest
tireless	finishes	useless	silently	thankful
lumpy	childish	classy	quicker	sixty
quickest	crunchy	amazement	stupidly	unlikely
fondness	requirement	defroster		

6.1 B Words

swinger	tireless	entirely	frankly	objective
enactment	hateful	refinement	lifeless	filthy
reflective	eventful	destructive	detachment	inconsistently
profitable	mindful	publisher	entrapment	protective
investment	selfless	witnesses	statement	detestable
establishment	limitless	instinctive	blankly	discontentment
novelty	drinker			

6.1 B Words (continued)

compactly	preventive	candidly	squelches	glossy
shoplifter	costly	shyly	neglectful	lanky
distinctly	enchantment	mildest	shadeless	requirement
funky	thankless	blissful	junky	embankment
trustful	vastly	risker	thriller	spunky
expandable	limpness	enrichment	insanely	boldly
plumpness	rudely	regretful	gruffest	slyly
crispy	retirement	sulky	prospective	fistful
useless	development	dresser	swelling	lonely
momently	stiffen	kindly	lameness	blemishing
crunches	remotely	refresher	prideful	impurely
zinger	boxes	detachment	sanely	abolishment
kinky	wilder	milder		

6.1 A Sentences

for   park   our

Steve acted impolite and childish.

Pete frequently finishes the job last.

The benches are cold and damp.

Get that plateful of ham sandwiches for dad.

There are sixty students in grade seven.

This old thing is useless!

Rosa was thankful Mrs. Chang has dependable help.

I will not go on the wildest amusement ride.

Cathy plans to be the fastest athlete.

Brenda is the strongest gal in the class.

Pete acted childish when he did not win the contest.

We will stop here for rest and refreshments.

I will chop a handful of nuts for the cupcakes.

Peg secretly wishes for a valentine from Jim.

The singer did not wish to compete.

That amusement park has the longest slide in the state.

Bill tells jokes for our amusement.

Jane is a dependable student.

Wendy is the strongest kid in our class.

6.1 B Sentences

about	Mrs.	does	for	her	into	because	you	could	our

Sandy was hopeful about the sales job.

The students were disrespectful to the substitute.

That film is such a thriller!

Dad is resting before he does the dishes.

The development of the economy in this state is strong.

The boss of my company is thankful.

I vote for the abolishment of that rule.

Frankly, I think that this junk is useless.

Bob plans to take that class as a refresher.

Mrs. Halpin was elected president of our club.

The volcano was destructive.

Bob went to get the refreshments.

This home is expandable, but it will be costly.

I think that this child is tireless!

The company must invest in dependable equipment.

Stan was lucky with the shipment.

Henry was grumpy when he had to prepare his taxes.

If you are not happy, the cost is refundable.

Jane candidly spoke to her mom.

I constantly use the defroster in the microwave.

It was such an eventful contest!

Jane wishes that she was hosting the next program.

If that volcano explodes, it can be extremely destructive.

We will promote the development of the product.

At this moment, I am entirely useless.

The cops had the shoplifter in handcuffs.

James is faster but he makes lots of mistakes.

The prospective sale is unlikely.

I selected to ignore his rudeness.

Beth is consistently risky with her cash.

The investment will not be profitable.

Is Jake the publisher of that script?

James was disrespectful to his boss.

The investment is unlikely.

This establishment frequently takes costly risks.

The singer thrills his thankful fans.

That childish statement was disrespectful.

James boldly told Sandy about his fondness for her.

That video was the longest thriller!

Tom was strongly suspected of shoplifting.

Frankly, I think that Beth is frequently late.

The kids disrupted the equipment.

The homesite is expandable to the west.

When I am neglectful, it is costly.

We must get that equipment to finish the job.

James thinks that Sally is protective.

6.2 A Words

/ed/

defrosted	distracted	expected	protested	defended
talented	protected	responded	insisted	disrupted
predicted	depended	intended	demanded	insulted
twisted	respected	prevented	requested	

/d/

filled	stalled	belonged	banged	filmed
thrilled	longed	called	spilled	swelled
skilled	smelled	drilled	spelled	killed

/t/

splashed	blinked	yanked	pressed	crunched
winked	stumped	jumped	camped	published
developed	thanked	punished	finished	thumped
demolished	dunked	limped	crossed	clamped
dressed	brushed	honked	wished	sniffed
established	stuffed	stamped		

6.2 B Words

/ed/

rejected	infested	expanded	impacted	inducted
detested	consisted	objected	contracted	erupted
consulted	convicted	disgusted	frequented	defected
openminded	implanted	resulted	concocted	suspected
obstructed				

/d/

mulled	recalled	billed	stilled	hulled
landfilled	willed	clanged	prolonged	jelled
bonged	hanged	dulled		

/t/

swished	bluffed	refreshed	banked	abolished
dumped	stashed	vanquished	chomped	basked
trashed	ranked	enriched	blemished	drenched
fluffed	handcuffed	stressed	published	famished
risked	flanked	punished	detached	clenched
bonked	clumped	clasped		

6.2 Nonsense

blished	frended	brilled	regrested	slunked
crinted	glomped	closhed	strinted	shonged
vabished	briffed	plinded	plashed	prilled

6.2 A Sentences

her	Mr.	they	would	after

/d/

Sally was thrilled to ride her bike.

Mr. Jones called on Steve in class.

The dentist drilled the cavity.

The truck stalled and came to a stop.

We filmed a video of the big event.

Sam smelled the rose then gave it to his mom.

The man filled the jugs behind the shed.

Henry filled his glass with the cold milkshake.

Ed spilled his hot drink on his tuxedo.

/t/

The man in the truck honked at the dog.

Kendra stamped the envelope.

Willy jumped up to get the candy.

Dave wished the game ended quickly.

That problem stumped the entire class.

The kids were punished when they broke the rules.

I splashed Mom when I jumped into the pond.

Gabe finished last but he did the best job.

The dog sniffed the bone in the dish.

Dad and the kids camped by the side of Magnum Lake.

/ed/   /t/   /d/

Jane twisted the lid off the jug.

We predicted that Sandra would win.

Mr. Long spelled his name for me.

I am thrilled to go to the basketball game.

Wendy developed her skill in track.

We brushed the dog after he had a bath.

Steve insulted his best pal by mistake.

I disrupted Dad and he was upset.

Sid camped alone with his dog.

6.2 B Sentences

Mrs.	for	after	out	away	about	every	new	her	snow

/d/

Beth longed for a ride in the red Mustang.

The clamplate smelled like the best fish dish.

Betsy was happy with the mold when it jelled.

Steve is quite skilled with his ability in welding.

Mrs. Jones filmed the event on video.

/d/

The company was billed for the shipment.

Jane is thrilled about the postponement of the banquet.

The bump must have dulled his wits.

We were hopeful after we mulled over the problem.

My leg swelled after it was hit by the ball.

/t/

Jake published his script.

Kendra was pressed for time.

Steve risked his life but he is safely out of the fire.

The debate was enriched by the tireless candidate.

Wendy bravely jumped in the cold lake.

The angry student clenched his fist.

Ken refreshed himself in the cold pond.

Dave limped for quite awhile after he fell.

Dad relished every moment with his children.

/ed/ *//t/* *//d/*

Bob wished that he had restricted the use of the equipment.

Steve defended his published script.

The boss requested more time for the skilled men.

Dad still wished to try clams.

Fred risked his life when he jumped from the plane.

We detached the wire from the TV.

Sandra felt refreshed after her bath.

Mr. Jones stressed that we must study.

Jim was thrilled with his trip to Calcutta.

Jane complimented Tommy on his wise investment.

Ed swished the ball into the basket.

Steve ranked fifth in the state contest.

/ed/   */t/*   */d/*

Dad inconsistently punished the kids.

The tot clenched his fists on the fast amusement ride.

The club will be established by June.

Frank detested it when the dentist drilled.

Jim frequently stashed his cash in secret spots.

6.3 A Words

usefulness	helpfulness	willingness	hopelessly	destructively
actively	skillfully	trustfully	restlessness	disrespectfully
hopefully	respectfully	helpfully	willingly	carelessly
wishfulness	thankfully	usefully		

6.3 B Words

effectively	endlessly	hatefully	neglectfully	lifelessly
tactlessly	fretfully	inventiveness	reflectively	objectively
mindfully	pridefully	protectively	effectiveness	freshened
sinfully	instinctively	uselessly	tirelessly	constructively
hatefulness	regretfully	expectingly	restfully	blissfully
tactfully	zestfully	sinfulness	fatefully	constructiveness
zestlessly	gratefully	distinctively	restlessly	selectively
spitefulness	thanklessness			

6.3 A Sentences

Ms.

Tim carelessly spilled the milk on the expensive rug.

Hopefully, we will go on a class trip in June.

Katy hit the softball skillfully.

Rod willingly helped Sandra with the job.

The dog jumped on the blocks destructively.

Fran<u>k</u> helpfully finished dusting the cobwebs.

Thankfully, I passed the last quiz.

Did the students stand respectfully?

The carelessness upset his mom.

<u>K</u>enny left the class disrespectfully.

6.3 B Sentences

for   doing   their   about

Bruno willingly went to help the candidate.

Ed and Babs tirelessly constructed their home.

James tossed restlessly in the bed.

Mom thanked the kids for helping with the dishes.

Neglectfully, Jason did not defrost the ham.

Betsy gratefully thanked her husband.

Restfully, Gram slept in the den.

Iva described the usefulness of this product.

Peg zestfully began the job.

Hopefully, Jan can go to the game.

<u>K</u>ate was optimistic about the prom.

Regretfully, Sandra will not compete in the contest.

The consultant must constructively develop a plan.

The band selectively chose songs for the banquet.

Stan pridefully told his dad about the win.

The basketball club zestfully defended their prize.

Sandra felt more confident when she dressed attractively.

apple	bugle	gobble	buckle	cuddle
fumble	tangle	scrabble	giggle	fizzle
bundle	fiddle	freckle	staple	ankle
crumble	snuggle	puddle	handle	tattle
twinkle	jumble	pickle	sniffle	sprinkle
gable	candle	hobble	wiggle	table
guzzle	trample	nibble	tackle	paddle
cradle	jingle	rattle	dimple	puzzle
raffle	juggle	thimble	sample	pebble
scribble	grumble	middle	simple	ripple
tickle	saddle	dazzle	topple	muzzle
ruffle	battle	able	tumble	dribble
dangle	scramble	little	single	jungle
stable	bottle	tremble	huddle	riddle
stumble	maple	sizzle	settle	struggle
drizzle	title	cable	rectangle	example

+s

apples	cuddles	giggles	freckles	ankles
snuggles	puddles	tattles	pickles	sniffles
sprinkles	wiggles	tables	cradles	rattles
puzzles	juggles	pebbles	scribbles	tickles
tumbles	jungles	huddles	riddles	maples
drizzles	settles	stables		

stle

castle	whistle	hustle

6.4 B Words

rubble	brittle	sable	joggle	frazzle
nettle	straddle	mingle	dabble	angle
razzle	meddle	cackle	gabble	pimple
grapple	stifle	muffle	baffle	coddle
bramble	jangle	griddle	babble	trickle
swizzle	prickle	humble	mantle	nuzzle
spindle	spittle	scruple	quibble	ruble
scuttle	shingle	mumble	rifle	addle
scuffle	dwindle	sickle	idle	nimble
ladle	kindle	spackle	fable	ramble
bangle	twiddle	fickle	haggle	trifle
noble	gamble	shackle	boggle	temple
duffle	bridle	muddle	straggle	entitle
embezzle	amble	bungle	grizzle	prattle
snuffle	dandle	heckle	unsettle	befuddle
subtitle	ventricle	unstable	multiple	cubicle
soluble	voluble	canticle	finagle	sensible
vehicle				

+s

joggles	dabbles	cackles	scruples	unsettles
bangles	vehicles	embezzles	gambles	stifles
scuttles	baffles	fables	trickles	mantles

stle

whistle	rustle	nestle	thistle	bustle
<u>wr</u>estle	castle	hustle	trestle	bristle
jostle	epistle	gristle	apostle	pestle

6.4 Nonsense

criggle	plondle	bozzle	ploble	chomdle
weggle	thumple	blittle	shrungle	biffle
muzle	flotle	stodle	spinkle	bleple

6.4 A Sentences

for   her   out   your   you

Jake will juggle with eggs!

We must try to get Tom to fumble the ball.

Henry will get the bundle in the van.

Do not disrupt the baby in the cradle.

The bottle is empty.

Hopefully, the paddle is not lost in the lake.

Drizzle is expected, so bring a hat.

A rectangle is the best shape for the cake.

Can you think of an example to demonstrate?

I did not fumble the ball when that tackle hit me.

You will find the saddle in the stable.

Kendra kindly gave the baby the rattle.

The singer is in the middle of her last song.

I think that riddle is hopeless.

Wendy willingly did the simple job.

Steve defended his title as champ.

Eva was thrilled to set the table with candles.

Mr. Long asked Tom to get the staples.

James carelessly fell in the puddle.

Sandra will gobble up her plateful of clams.

There are still lots of animals in the jungle.

This spelling quiz is not simple at all.

Bring your fiddle and bugle to band class.

The kids can help get the bundles out of the van.

The class will hold a raffle to get some cash.

Sprinkle a handful of nuts on the cake.

Did you stumble on that little pebble?

It is a struggle to finish this puzzle.

6.4 B Sentences

		out	over	could	you	does

The club must hold a raffle to make some cash.

Those kids quibble over the smallest things!

Could you staple and file these documents?

The sample will hopefully get us sales.

Sheldon broke his leg so he hobbles up the steps.

Jimmy hopes that he will be able to get that expensive van.

The second baseman did not like to mingle with the fans.

Beth was idle and felt she was useless.

We must haggle before we make the deposit.

This company had to struggle to get established here.

Tom had a dimple in his chin.

Mom told Sam to get his bugle.

This win will entitle me to the grand prize contest.

We must finagle a plan to get us out of this mess!

Bring multiple samples to the shop.

I think that the baby will resemble me!

Did Mr. Jones embezzle the cash?

Mom will make the swing set stable.

stle

Did Henry whistle rudely to the boss?

Hopefully, we will visit the castle.

Jane must hustle to get the <u>k</u>ids to the bus on time!

The pup was thankful for the gristle.

Dad rapidly develops bristle when he does not shave.

That thistle plant should be in the sun.

The job will require a trestle.